A to Zoo

26 TEACHABLE ANIMAL TALES

JOE CONROY

Published in the United States of America

ISBN 978-1-960684-26-4 (SC)
ISBN 978-1-960684-24-0 (HC)
ISBN 978-1-960684-25-7 (Ebook)

Joe Conroy Publishing, LLC.
Contact@atozoobook.com
www.animallearningnetwork.com

Order Information and Rights Permission:

Quantity sales. Special discounts might be available on quantity purchases by corporations, associations, and others. For details, contact the publisher at the address above.

For Book Rights Adaptation and other Rights Permission.
Call us at toll-free 1-888-945-8513 or send us an email at admin@stellarliterary.com.

To my beautiful wife Kelly, your loving support and encouragement has made this and all my dreams come true.

Contents

Artie the Aardvark

Artie loved playing baseball. He went to the park to see if he could find someone to play with. None of the kids had ever seen an aardvark before, so they were a little surprised by his long nose. Artie looked different, and that made them nervous.

The first team Artie saw as he walked into the park were the raccoons. They were playing on the front field. Artie ran over to see if he could join them. When he got closer, Artie shouted, "Hey, guys, can I play with you?"

The raccoons took one look at Artie and said, "No way, long nose. We don't want someone who looks like you on our team. Go bother someone else."

Artie's feelings were hurt, but he wasn't going to give up. The dogs were playing on the next field. They look friendly, maybe I can play with them, thought Artie. He ran up to the fence and said, "Hey, guys, can I play on your team?"

Artie was about to tell them what a good pitcher he was when Doug shouted, "No way, you look funny. We don't want any funny looking people on our team, right guys?"

"Right, go away funny face," said the other dogs and they laughed at poor Artie.

Artie ran off, feeling sad, but he loved baseball so much that he kept trying to find a team to play with. He asked the rabbits and the chipmunks and even the badgers, but the answer was always the same.

Nobody wanted him on their team because he looked different. Artie was about to give up when he saw the foxes playing on the south field. He decided to give it one more try. Unfortunately, the foxes were the meanest of all.

"Hey, guys, my name is Artie, and I'm a really good pitcher. Can I play with you?" he asked.

"No way. We don't want a long nose like you on our team!" shouted Fred.

"I know why he's such a good pitcher," said Frankie. "Because one look at that nose and you'd be laughing too hard to hit the ball."

The foxes burst out laughing. Artie felt terrible and ran away to the top of the hill to be by himself. While Artie sat on the top of the hill with his head on his knees, he didn't see the squirrels come into the park. When Artie finally picked his head up, he saw the squirrels were playing on the backfield.

Artie became so interested in the squirrel's game that he forgot about being sad. Sam, their best player, grabbed his bat and stepped up to the plate. Steve pitched a fastball, and Sam swung with all his might, knocking the ball over the fence. The ball bounced across the street, slid over the ledge, and rolled into a deep narrow hole.

The squirrels tried to get the ball, but the hole was just too deep. Without their ball, they couldn't play anymore. Then they saw Artie running down the hill.

A little out of breath, Artie said, "I saw what happened. Do you need some help?"

"Sure," said Sam, "our ball is stuck in that hole and we can't reach it. Without our ball, we can't play anymore and have to go home."

Artie looked into the hole, and it was so dark he couldn't see the ball. "You're right, that hole is deep," said Artie, "but I'll give it a try." Artie lay down on his stomach and stretched his nose into the hole. He was stretching pretty far and started to think that maybe the hole was too deep, even for him. Then all of a sudden, he felt it. Artie grabbed the ball, pulled it out of the hole, and raised it high into the air.

The squirrels jumped and cheered. "He did it! Artie saved the ball! Yeah!"

"I can't believe you reached that," said Sam. "That was great. Thanks a lot. If it weren't for you, I don't know what we would have done. Hey, do you want to play with us?"

Artie couldn't believe it. Sam had just asked him to play baseball. He was so excited, but then he remembered about his nose. Artie's head lowered in disappointment as he asked, "Are you sure? Doesn't my nose bother you?"

"Are you kidding? We love that nose!" said Sam. "That nose saved our baseball! Now grab your stuff and let's play some ball!"

Artie picked up his mitt and ran off to play baseball with his new friends. The squirrels soon realized that Artie's nose was good for something else—pitching. Artie turned out to be the best pitcher in the whole league. The other kids felt bad about the way they treated Artie and apologized for it. Artie was so happy playing baseball that he couldn't be mad at anyone. Now the squirrels, with Artie pitching, are in first place, and they love Artie—long nose and all.

Billy the Bear

Billy was bored. He spent the whole morning wandering around the forest looking for something fun to do. When he got to the north field he saw Betty the bunny, Sally the squirrel and Rickey the raccoon playing with Sally's brand new red ball.

"Sally, pass me the ball," said Betty, "watch what I can do."

Betty caught the ball and balanced it on her nose. Then she hopped high into the air without dropping the ball.

"Wow, that was really great," said Ricky. "Can I try?"

Betty tossed the ball to Ricky. He got it balanced on his nose, but when he tried to hop, he tripped over a branch and fell backward into a huge pile of leaves. It was really funny, and the three of them laughed about it for a long time.

Billy sat at the edge of the field, watching them have a great time. Billy didn't understand why they never asked him to play. He liked to play ball. He was really good at hopping around while balancing a ball on his nose. The more he thought about being left out, the madder he got. Billy became so mad that he couldn't take it anymore. Billy decided if he couldn't play ball, then neither could they, and he let out a huge growl.

"Oh no, it's Billy," shouted Ricky. "Quick, everyone, run and hide!"

Billy came crashing through the trees, growling, and running straight at them. Sally was so scared that she dropped her new shiny red ball and ran away as fast as she could. They hid behind the big rock and watched as Billy picked up Sally's ball and squished it with his big sharp claws.

Sally was very upset. She got that ball as a birthday present from her favorite uncle. "Oh, why does Billy always have to be so mean?" sobbed Sally.

"I don't know why, Sally," said Betty, "but I'm getting pretty tired of Billy ruining everything. It's time someone stood up to him. Come on, follow me."

Ricky and Sally followed behind Betty as she headed towards Billy. Betty was really mad at Billy, but the closer she got to him, the more afraid she became. Billy was very big and scary looking, but someone had to stand up to him. So, Betty gathered up her courage and hopped right up to Billy and said, "Billy, that was very mean! Why did you break Sally's ball? We didn't do anything to you!"

"Well, I saw you playing ball and having lots of fun. I like to play ball, but no-one ever asks me to play, and that makes me really mad," growled Billy. "So, I broke the ball!"

"Do you know why no one wants to play with you?" asked Betty. "It's because you are always mean to people. Maybe if you stop growling and scaring everyone, people would play with you. Now apologize to Sally for breaking her ball."

Billy felt bad for what he had done. "Sally, I'm sorry for breaking your ball. I know it's no excuse but watching you guys play made me feel really left out. The more I watched, the worse it got. It made me so crazy that I just couldn't take it anymore. I'm sorry I broke your ball. I promise I will get you a new one."

Sally felt bad for Billy. "That's okay, Billy, I understand. It wasn't very nice of us not to ask you to play. We're sorry for leaving you out and hurting your feelings. I know it might be a little late, but would you like to play with us now?"

Billy couldn't believe it! After everything he had done, Sally still asked him to play. "Really? I would love to play with you guys!" smiled Billy. The four of them ran off into the woods to play hide and go seek for the rest of the day.

Billy kept his promise to Sally and got her a brand-new shiny red ball. From then on, they played together almost every day. They had lots of fun and soon became the best of friends. Now that Billy is nice to everyone, he has lots of new friends to play with, and that makes him very happy.

Cathy the Cat

Cathy lived on a farm in the country. She loved living in the barn with all the other animals. Every night, she would climb to the top loft and fall asleep in the hay. Each morning when she woke up, Cathy washed herself off and climbed back down.

Colleen, a motherly old cow, always had plenty of fresh milk for Cathy to drink. It was a great life living in the barn. One day, loud grunting noises woke Cathy up from her nap. She raced downstairs to find out what it was. Colleen told her that Farmer Fred just arrived with a truckload of pigs.

"Why pigs?" said Colleen. "They're dirty and make a mess out of everything. Now, Cathy, you stay away from them. They're nothing but trouble."

Cathy had never seen a pig before and couldn't wait to meet one. When she slipped out of the barn, the pigs were gone. She couldn't see them anywhere and decided to go look for them. While walking through the cornfield, Cathy heard the same strange grunting noises she heard earlier. It must be the pigs, she thought and ran as fast as she could towards the sound. When she burst out of the cornfield, the pigs were all cooped up in a pen. Slowly, Cathy walked up to the pen and said, "Hello, my name is Cathy. What's your name?"

"Hello, Cathy," answered one of the pigs, "my name is Peter. What are you doing way out here, so far away from the barn?"

"I heard that Farmer Fred had brought some new people to the farm and I wanted to meet you. I love making new friends, but by the time I came out of the barn, you were gone. So I decided to look for you, and now I've found you. What I don't understand is why you are way out here and not in the barn with everyone else."

"Farmer Fred would never let us sleep in the barn," said Peter. "He says we are too dirty and would mess up his nice clean barn."

Cathy thought about it for a minute and said, "I know, why don't we get you cleaned up and then maybe Farmer Fred will let you live in the barn?"

"That sounds like a great idea!" said Peter. "The only problem is that we don't know how to get clean or stay clean. We're pigs. No one has ever shown us how."

"Oh, that's easy," said Cathy. "I can show you how to take a bath and wash yourselves. It's really easy and lots of fun getting clean."

Cathy explained how they needed to take a bath every day. She taught them to wash their hands and face before they ate. She got them to wash their hands when they went to the bathroom. Peter and the rest of the pigs even started keeping the pen clean.

One day, while Cathy was on her way to see Peter, she heard Farmer Fred talking to his wife. He told her he had never seen such clean pigs in his entire life. He told her that if they kept this up, next month he would move them into the barn.

Cathy couldn't wait to tell Peter the good news. She ran as fast as she could through the cornfield and straight to the pen. "Peter, guess what?" she said, a little out of breath. "I just heard Farmer Fred tell his wife that if you keep staying clean, next month he'll move you into the barn. Isn't that great news?"

"Yes, that would be great!" said Peter. "We've never lived in a nice warm barn before. What about the other animals? Are you sure they won't mind?"

Now Cathy knew that some of the animals didn't like pigs, but that was because they didn't know them like she did. Cathy said, "I'm sure once they see how neat and clean you are, they will love you guys."

The pigs did keep clean, and Farmer Fred was true to his word and moved the pigs into the barn. Now with all the pigs helping keep the barn nice and neat, cleaning is easy. They are so neat and clean that even Colleen has learned to like them.

Now that the pigs are living in the barn, everyone is happy, especially Cathy. She loves having all her friends in the barn with her. Peter and the other pigs are the happiest, because they get to live in the warm barn with good friends. And it's all because they're clean and not dirty.

Dozey the Dog

Dozey lives in a house by the woods. Her brother, Dasher, is always running around the house making their mom crazy.

Her sister, Dawn, is quiet and likes to wake up early and watch the sun rise. Dozey has a hard time waking up, because she is not very good about going to bed on time. Dozey likes to stay up late, watching TV, or playing with her toys. Her parents try to explain why she needs to go to bed early and get plenty of rest, but unfortunately, Dozey hasn't learned that lesson yet.

Monday, after work, Dozey's dad, Daniel, came home with some really great news. "Guess what I got today?" said Daniel as he dropped a bunch of tickets on the table. "That's right! Front row tickets to the big circus on Saturday!"

The kids couldn't believe it! Front row seats; this was going to be great! Dozey was so excited that she could barely contain herself. The next week seemed like it lasted forever. It was finally Friday night, and the kids were watching TV, when Mom came in.

"Okay, everyone," Mom said, "time for bed. Tomorrow's the big day. Remember what your dad said. We need to be ready to leave the house by seven or we'll miss the show. That means up at 6:00 a.m. That will give you enough time get ready, eat breakfast, and be ready to leave by 7:00 a.m. Now off to bed," said their mom.

The kids ran upstairs, put on their pajamas, brushed their teeth, and were in bed in record time. Dasher and Dawn were asleep by the time their mom came to check on them. However, Dozey was playing pretend circus with her dolls. "Dozey," her mom said, "put those dolls away and go to sleep."

About an hour later, Mom checked on them and found Dozey wide awake, playing with her dolls. Mom was not too happy and she took her dolls away and said, "Dozey, you need to go to sleep, it's way past bedtime. If you don't get some sleep, you'll never be able to wake up, and you will miss the circus. Now go to sleep." She turned off the light and closed the door.

Dozey tried for five minutes to fall asleep but couldn't, so she snuck out of bed, got some new toys and began playing circus again.

About half an hour later, Dozey heard footsteps and her door opened slowly. It was her dad, and not wanting to get in trouble, Dozey pretended she was asleep. Once he was gone, Dozey pulled out her dolls and began playing circus again. Dozey thought she could play a little longer and still get up in time for the circus; but she was wrong.

At 6:00 a.m., her dad came in and said, "Good morning! Time to get up. We have a big day ahead of us."

Dasher and Dawn were so excited for the circus, they jumped out of bed and got dressed as fast as they could. Dozey was so tired that she just couldn't get up. I just need five more minutes, she thought and fell asleep before her head hit the pillow.

"Come on, Dozey," said Dawn, "wake up. We're going to the circus!" "Ugh, leave me alone," grumbled Dozey and she fell back asleep.

Dozey's parents tried and tried, but they just couldn't wake Dozey up. It was seven o'clock and they couldn't wait any longer. They called Grandma and she came over to watch Dozey while the rest of the family went to the circus.

When Dozey finally woke up, she looked at the clock and it said 10:30 a.m. Oh, no! panicked Dozey, that can't be right. They were leaving at 7:00 a.m. for the circus. The clock must be broken, thought

Dozey and she ran downstairs just to be sure. Dozey was surprised to see her grandma sitting in a chair reading a book.

Dozey realized that something was wrong and asked, "Grandma, what are you doing here? Where is everyone? We're supposed to go to the circus today."

"Come sit with me," her grandma said, patting the seat right next to her. "I've got some bad news for you. No one is here. They left for the circus hours ago. They tried to wake you up many times, but you just wouldn't get up."

"They what?" shouted Dozey. "They left me? How could they do that to me?"

"Now, hold on, Dozey," said Grandma, "they didn't do this to you. It's not their fault that you wouldn't wake up. Your mom told you several times to go to bed, but you chose to stay up late and play with your dolls. I'm sorry, but it's your fault that you missed the circus, not theirs."

Dozey thought about it for a few minutes and said, "Oh, Grandma, you're right. I can't believe I missed the circus. It's all my fault," said Dozey as she laid her head down in her grandma's lap and began to cry.

"I know, honey," said Grandma, gently stroking her hair. "This is really hard on you, but you'll get through it. I hope you learned your lesson so it won't happen again."

"Oh, I learned my lesson," said Dozey as she hugged her grandma.

From then on, when her parents said it was bedtime, Dozey was the first one to go to bed. She doesn't stay up late anymore, so waking up in the morning is easy. Dozey is much happier now because she wakes up with lots of energy and never misses a thing. She gets to go to the circus and do lots of fun things all because she goes to sleep when her parents say it's bedtime.

Ellie the Elephant

Ellie always dreamed of having long beautiful tusks. Her mom told her that one day soon, her tusks would grow. Ellie just couldn't wait, and each morning, she checked in the mirror to see if they started to grow. A week later, it finally happened—Ellie saw a tusk growing. She was so excited, she ran to her mom, and shouted, "Mom, Mom, guess what? My tusks are starting to grow! Look, Look!"

"Oh, that's wonderful!" her mom said. "I'm so happy for you. Now remember what we talked about—having tusks is a big responsibility. You need to keep them clean all day long if you want them to grow big and strong. Come on, let's go to the bathroom and I'll show you what to do."

Her mom handed Ellie the brush and said, "It's important that you clean the whole tusk and not just the front part. You need to brush the top and bottom and all around the sides and don't forget about the tip. It's very important to get all the dirt off. The best way to do that is to make little circles with your brush. After that, you go up and down, like this," said her mom as she showed Ellie how to brush. "Now all you need to do is rinse off and you are done."

Ellie's mom watched her practice brushing her tusks. Ellie had some trouble at first, but after a few tries, she got the hang of it. Her mom explained that it was important to keep them clean all day long. She needed to brush when she got up and again at bedtime. "If you want them to grow big and strong, then remember to brush them after every meal."

Her mom was right that taking care of tusks was a lot of work, but it was worth it. Ellie was just so happy to have tusks. "Don't worry, Mom, I will take really good care of them," promised Ellie. "Now, can I go show my friends my new tusks?"

"Sure, go show your friends," said her mom. "Just be home in time for dinner."

Ellie ran off to show her friends her new tusks. She was so excited that she showed them to everyone she met. On her way home, Ellie realized she forgot to show Uncle Edgar her tusks. She ran to his house and knocked on his front door. Ellie knocked again, but no one answered. As she was about to leave, she thought she heard someone crying. The door was open, so Ellie stuck her head inside and called, "Uncle Edgar? It's me, Ellie. Can I come in?"

Ellie walked to the kitchen where she heard someone crying. She slowly opened the kitchen door, and there was Uncle Edgar, sitting at the table with his head in his hands, gently sobbing.

"What's wrong, Uncle Edgar?" asked Ellie.

"Hi, Ellie," said Uncle Edgar as he wiped away his tears. "I'm not doing so good. Yesterday at work, one of my tusks broke in half."

"That's terrible! What can I do?" asked Ellie. "Do you need a dentist?"

"That's very sweet of you, Ellie, but I went yesterday," said Uncle Edgar. The dentist said there was nothing he could do. He told me my tusk broke because I didn't do a good job taking care of them when I was young. He said my tusks were very big but not very strong. Maybe if I did a better job of cleaning while they were growing, this might not have happened. Now don't you worry about me, I will be fine. Tell me, why did you come to see me?"

"Well, I just wanted to show you that my tusks are starting to grow," said Ellie.

"That's so exciting," said Uncle Edgar. "I'm happy for you, but promise me that you'll take good care of your tusks. I never want anything like this to happen to you."

"I promise to take good care of them," said Ellie. She stayed and talked with Uncle Edgar for a long time. Ellie looked at the clock and saw that it was getting late. "Well, I better get going. Mom said I need to be home in time for dinner. Bye, Uncle Edgar, I'm sorry about your tusk. I hope you feel better. I love you," Ellie said as she hugged him goodbye.

"Bye, Ellie," said Uncle Edgar, "congratulations on your tusks. Take good care of them and say hello to your mom for me."

"I will," said Ellie as she walked out the front door and made her way home.

When Ellie got home, she went straight to the bathroom and brushed her tusks. Her mom was so proud of her. In fact, over the next few years, Ellie took better care of her tusks than any other elephant. Now that they are fully-grown, Ellie has the strongest best-looking tusks of all the elephants and that makes her very happy.

21

Freddy the Frog

Freddy loved to jump. His favorite thing to jump on was his bed. When his mom caught him jumping on the good couch, she got mad.

"Freddy! Stop jumping on the furniture," his mom yelled. "How many times do I have to tell you? No jumping on the furniture. If you want to jump, go outside and do it, unless you would prefer to spend the day in your room?

"Sorry, Mom," said Freddy and he ran outside as fast as he could.

Outside, Freddy was free to jump on or over whatever he wanted. He loved making jumping contests. He played for hours with his friends jumping over bushes and landing on the lily pads. Once he even tried to jump over the pond, but he didn't make it. His mom was not too happy when he went inside and got everything soaking wet.

One day while Freddy was setting up a jumping course his dad asked if he wanted to help pick out the new family car. Freddy was so excited that he dropped what he was doing and raced his dad to the car where his mom was waiting for them. Before he could even sit down his mom said, "Freddy, make sure your seat belt is on, and no jumping around, we don't want any accidents."

"Oh, Mom," whined Freddy, "why do I always have to put on my seat belt? Every time we get in the car, you say, 'Freddy, put on your seat belt.' I hate my seatbelt. It chokes me."

"Freddy, stop complaining," his mom said. "You need to wear your seat belt so nothing bad happens. If we were in an accident, that seat belt could save your life. Now stop whining and put it on."

Freddy put it on and soon forgot all about his seat belt as he dreamed of a new car. When they turned into the dealership there were cars everywhere. Red ones and blue ones and big green ones and small black ones that went super-fast. It took forever but they finally found the perfect car. It was a white convertible way in the back.

It was the perfect size, not too fast but not too slow either. Everyone loved the white convertible and they decided to buy it. While waiting for his dad to do the paperwork, Freddy jumped all over exploring the new car. Every few minutes it was the same.

All excited Freddy said, "Mom, look how cool this is."

"That's nice Freddy," his mom replied, not even looking up from the magazine she was flipping through.

Freddy must have said "look mom" a hundred times before the door opened and his dad hopped in. He jingled the keys high in the air, smiled and said, "Who wants to go for a convertible ride?"

"I do, I do," said Freddy and got so excited asking, "Can I push the button, please, please, please?"

"Sorry adults only," said his mom. Then with a big smile, "Well maybe just this one time."

"Thanks mom, you're the best!" said Freddy and he hopped into the front seat. When he pushed the button, it was like magic. The top went straight up into the air and came back down all folded up. It was the coolest thing Freddy had ever seen. "I have a magic robot car" thought Freddy when he heard his mother's voice. "Freddy the tops down, you did a great job, but now I need you to do an equally great job of sitting in your seat and putting on your seatbelt."

Freddy was so happy to ride in their new car that he didn't even complain about putting on his seatbelt. He watched the buckle click into place and when he picked his head up to look out, that's when it happened. Freddy couldn't see out. No matter how far he stretched his neck he couldn't see over the folded-up top. Freddy was so disappointed; they finally got a cool new magic robot car, and he couldn't see out. Oh no! What was he going to do? His mind raced for a solution. That's when the craziest idea popped into his head. What if he took off his seatbelt and did a little jump? Nothing too big. Just high enough to see over the top. was so focused on seeing out that he forgot about the danger of not wearing a seatbelt.

So, before his dad started to drive away Freddy went for it. He popped off his seatbelt and jumped. Unfortunately, it was a much stronger jump than he had planned. He went soaring into the air and for one second, he could see for miles, then gravity took hold, and he came crashing back down. With a loud thump Freddy landed face up in the back seat.

Worried he was hurt, his parents asked, "Freddy are you alright?"

Rubbing his head, Freddy managed to say, "I think so," but quickly realized he made a big mistake and thought his parents would mad.

But instead, his mom said in a very calm voice, "Freddy, I'm so happy you are okay. You know we love you but taking off your seatbelt is never a good idea. I hate to think about what might have happened if we were moving," and she couldn't finish her sentence and two little tears ran down her face.

"Mom, I'm really sorry I scared you guys like that. I scared myself too. I promise I will never, ever, ever take my seatbelt off again."

Freddy kept his promise and from then on, he always wore his seatbelt and was a lot safer and a lot happier because of it.

Gracie the Goat

Gracie's life on the farm was great. Each morning, Farmer Frank would put food out for all his animals to eat. There were lots of oats and grains to help them grow big and strong. He also gave them plenty of fruits and vegetables to keep them healthy. Farmer Frank loved his animals and did his best to take good care of them.

There were many different animals that lived on his farm. Most of them loved to eat all the wonderful things that Farmer Frank would give them. Some days, there were yummy carrots; and other days, they had string beans or peas. Every Friday, as a special treat, Farmer Frank gave them corn on the cob. Everyone loved to eat the corn because it came fresh from the fields.

Gracie was the only goat on the farm. She was orphaned at a very young age and never had anyone to teach her the benefits of eating healthy. She grew up eating only things with lots of sugar in them. She would eat candy and junk food she would find in the woods. The problem with Gracie was that she refused to try anything that was good for her. She thought it would taste bad, so she refused to eat it.

While the other animals were eating the delicious healthy food, Gracie would sneak off into the woods. She would go to the campgrounds and eat all the candy wrappers and soda cans left by the kids.

One day, while munching on his carrots, Harry, the big strong plow horse, noticed that Gracie wasn't eating anything, and asked, "Gracie, why aren't you eating your carrots? Are you all right?"

"I'm fine," said Gracie. "I don't want any. They look yucky, and I won't eat them."

"Have you ever tried them?" asked Henry.

"Not exactly, but I can tell that they taste bad and I won't like them," said Gracie.

"How do you know what they taste like if you haven't even tried them?" asked Harry. "I love carrots. They're so crunchy and delicious. Besides, don't you know that you have to eat fruits and vegetables every day if you want to stay healthy?"

"I'm perfectly healthy and I don't eat any fruits or vegetables. Anyway, you're not my dad, and you can't make me eat them," said Gracie, and she ran off to the campgrounds to look for more candy.

Who does he think he is? thought Gracie. Harry's not the boss of me. I don't have to eat anything that I don't want to. I've been eating candy and soda my whole life and I'm perfectly fine. Silly old horse. He doesn't know what he's missing. Gracie gobbled up the candy wrapper she just found.

About a month later, while feeding the animals, Farmer Frank saw Gracie lying down on the ground. That's odd, thought Frank, and he went over to see what was going on. He went to her and saw that Gracie looked sick and was holding her stomach. Farmer Frank quickly called the doctor to see if he could help her.

The doctor took one look at Gracie and knew she was very sick. He picked Gracie up and put her into the back of his truck and took her straight to the animal hospital. They had to give Gracie a shot and some very bad tasting medicine to help her tummy ache get better. From eating all that junk food, Gracie's stomach was all red and irritated. She had to stay in the hospital for seven days before her stomach felt good enough to go home.

The doctor explained that the reason she felt so sick was because she ate too much junk food and not enough healthy food. If she didn't start eating her fruits and vegetables soon, this was going to happen again. Gracie's belly hurt so bad that she never wanted to feel like this ever again.

"Oh, Doctor," Gracie said, "I promise I'll never eat junk food again and will only eat fruits and vegetables from now on."

"Candy every now and then is okay," explained the doctor. "You just can't eat it all the time. Your body needs fruits and vegetables and other healthy things for it to work properly. If you eat healthy foods every day, then you won't get as sick as often."

From then on, Gracie ate her fruits and vegetables every day. Now that she eats healthy, Gracie feels better and hardly ever gets sick. She even has more energy for running and playing with her friends. Gracie feels great, and it's all because she eats less candy and more fruits and vegetables.

Heidi the Hyena

Heidi felt great! The sun was shining and a cool breeze was blowing as she strolled through the woods on her way to the park. Life was just perfect; how could anyone not be happy on a day like this? Out of the corner of her eye, Heidi saw someone running. It looks like Molly the mongoose, she thought, but it can't be. Everyone is meeting at the swings in ten minutes and that's not the way to the swings. So Heidi turned and went after her friend. Heidi followed the trail of broken branches to the clearing by the big elm tree. There was Molly, curled up in a ball, leaning against the tree, crying softly.

"What's the matter, Molly?" asked Heidi as she went to her friend's side.

"Heidi, what are you doing here?" Molly was surprised to see Heidi. "Why aren't you at the swings with everyone else?"

"I was on my way there when I saw you running off in the wrong direction," said Heidi. "I just wanted to make sure that everything is okay."

"That's really nice of you," said Molly. "That's why everyone likes you." Molly's eyes began to tear up. "Why don't they like me? I try really hard to be nice, but does anyone want to be my best friend? No, everyone wants to be your best friend. It's not fair. Why don't they like me?"

"That's not true, Molly, the other kids like you. I like you," said Heidi. "It's just that sometimes you can be a little negative. Nobody wants to play with someone who's always complaining about something. I bet if you stopped being so negative, the other kids would want to play with you. I'll let you in on a secret. When we first moved here, I didn't know anyone. The first two weeks of school were just awful. No one talked to me, and I had to eat lunch all by myself. I thought I would never have a friend and be alone for the rest of my life. That's when my mom told me the secret to making friends."

"The what?" asked Molly. "There's a secret to making friends? Oh, Heidi, you just have to tell me the secret! Oh, please tell me how I get the other kids to like me!"

"Well, it's going to sound a little silly, but it really works," said Heidi.

"Tell me, tell me," said Molly, "I don't care if it's silly. I'll do anything"

"Okay, my mom said that the secret to making friends was to be happy, put a smile on your face, and be nice. I thought my mom was crazy when she told me that, but I didn't have any friends, so I decided to give it a try. So for the next week, I smiled at everyone and had a happy attitude, even when I didn't feel happy. Then one day, Helen came up to me and said she liked me because I was always happy. Then before I knew it, I became friends with everyone in the neighborhood," said Heidi.

"You're right, Heidi, it does sound a little silly. How is putting a smile on my face and being happy going to get people to like me?" asked Molly.

"I'm not sure how it works," said Heidi. "I think it's because people would rather be around someone happy and not someone grouchy."

Molly still wasn't sure about Heidi's idea, but it did make sense, so she decided to give it a try. Molly and Heidi took off for the playground to test out their idea.

Molly, with Heidi by her side, walked up to a group of kids that were sitting on the park bench, swinging their feet back and forth, looking very bored. Molly put on her best smile and in her happiest voice said, "Hi, what are you guys doing?"

"Hi, Heidi. Hi, Molly," the kids said, sounding sad. "We're bored. There is nothing to do, so we're just hanging out."

"Well, I think I'm going to play on the swings. Anyone want to join me?" asked Molly with a great big smile on her face.

"I don't know. It doesn't look like much fun," grumbled the kids.

Molly was disappointed but kept the smile on her face and ran off to the swings. She hopped on the swing, and in seconds, she was pretty high. Molly began giggling and laughing, sounding like she was having the time of her life. The other kids walked over to the swings to see what was going on.

"Mind if we join you?" asked the kids as they climbed on the empty swings.

"Sure, the more people, the more fun!" said Molly. They played for hours and had the best time. They had so much fun that the kids asked if Molly wanted to go to the skate park with them tomorrow. Molly couldn't believe it! The other kids actually wanted to be with her. At that moment, Molly realized that Heidi was right. She ran over and gave Heidi a big hug, whispering in her ear, "Thank you so much!"

"You're welcome." Heidi smiled as she hugged her friend. Now Molly has lots of friends, and it's all because she put a smile on her face and happiness in her heart, just like her best friend, Heidi.

Iggy the Iguana

Iggy's favorite thing to do was go to the beach. He loved to lie on the sand and soak up the sun. The best part was the warm feeling he got all over his body while sunbathing. One night at dinner, Iggy's dad said, "I've got a big surprise for everyone. Next week, during spring break, we are going on a family vacation." "Really? Where are we going?" asked Iggy.

"We're spending a week at the equator," his dad said. "We're staying at the Sunshine Resort, right on the beach. The resort has all kinds of great things to do. Would you like to see some pictures?"

"Yes, I've always wanted to go to the equator. Thanks, Mom and Dad!" said Iggy, jumping up and down.

For the next week, all Iggy could think about was his vacation. The resort looked great. It had volleyball and tennis. There was sailing and windsurfing and just about everything you could think of. One day, there was a parade. Another night, they had a Hawaiian Luau with hula dancers and fire-eaters. There was something great going on every day. The best part was that it was hot and sunny all the time. Iggy couldn't wait to lie in the sun. It was warm where he lived, but nothing like the equator. This was one of the hottest places on Earth, and Iggy was sure this was going to be the best vacation ever.

Iggy couldn't wait. It seemed like forever, but finally the day came for them to leave for vacation. When they got off the plane, a big fancy bus took them to the resort. The place was even better than he had imagined. They ate dinner in the Waterfall Café and decided to turn in early as they were all tired from the long day of traveling.

"We know you like to wake up early," said Iggy's mom. "If you leave us a note, you can go to the beach, and only the beach, if you are up before we are."

Iggy was up at sunrise and he could hear the beach calling his name. So he wrote his mom and dad a note, grabbed his towel, and headed off to the beach.

About an hour later, Iggy's mom showed up. "Iggy, you forgot your suntan lotion," she said, handing him the bottle. "Remember what we talked about. The sun is hotter here, and you need to use plenty of lotion or you will get a really bad sunburn. Your father and I are going on the bus tour. Would you like to come with us or stay here?"

"I would rather stay on the beach, if that's okay with you," said Iggy.

"Okay, you're old enough, but remember the rules—no leaving the resort, there is plenty of food and water in the room. Don't forget, suntan lotion at least once every hour," said his mom as she kissed him goodbye. "I love you. Have fun and we'll see you in a few hours."

"Bye, Mom, don't worry, I'll be fine. Maybe tonight we can all go to the Hawaiian luau?" said Iggy as he waved goodbye to his mom.

Iggy couldn't believe it. He had a whole day of just lying on the beach. The sun was really strong, just the way he liked it. Before long, Iggy felt the warmth of the sun all over his body and it felt great! Iggy decided to wait a little longer before putting on the suntan lotion. It made him feel sweaty and he didn't like it very much. After a little while, Iggy was so warm and relaxed that he slowly drifted off to sleep.

When his parents returned, they found Iggy fast asleep on the beach. One look at him and they knew he was in trouble. Iggy's back was a dark red, almost purple, and he had tiny white blisters all over. When Iggy woke up, he was in so much pain that he could barely move. His parents rushed him to the resort doctor. He examined Iggy and said that he had second-degree burns on his back and it was very serious.

The doctor put special burn cream on his back and gave him some medicine for the pain. Unfortunately, there was little else he could do for Iggy. He would have to stay out of the sun until his body healed.

Iggy felt horrible. His back was on fire and it hurt just to put a shirt on. He stayed in bed for the rest of the vacation. He missed the Hawaiian luau and the parades. He missed out on the beautiful beaches and the wonderful things the resort had to offer.

Iggy couldn't believe it—his perfect vacation was ruined, all because he didn't put on suntan lotion! It took months for his back to completely heal, and he decided he would never let that happen again. Now that Iggy uses suntan lotion the right way, he doesn't get burned and has never missed a day of fun in the sun again.

Jackie the Jaguar

Jackie was a very fast runner, and she loved everything to do with running. Each day after school, she would run home as fast as she could, trying to beat the previous days' time.

"Hi, Jackie," her mom said. "How was school today? Learn anything new?"

"School was fine," answered Jackie as she threw her book bag in the corner and asked, "Can I go out and play now?"

Her mom gave her the "mother look" and said, "First, you can pick up that book bag and put it where it belongs. Then you can go upstairs, do your homework, and change into play clothes. When you are done with all that, you may go out to play."

Jackie grabbed her bag, ran upstairs, changed her clothes, and did her homework as fast as she could. "Mom, I'm done with my homework, can I go play now?" she yelled as she headed towards the front door. "I'm supposed to meet Joseph and Jessica at the big field by four o'clock. We need to practice for the big race on Saturday. I just know if I practice every day, I can win," said Jackie.

Jackie's mom checked her homework and said, "Okay, you may go now. Have fun with your friends, but make sure you look both ways when crossing the street, and be home in time for dinner."

"Thanks, Mom," said Jackie as she kissed her on the cheek and ran out the door.

Jackie was careful and looked both ways as she crossed the streets to get to the big field. Joseph and Jessica were already there, and they were happy to see their friend.

"Hi, Jackie," they said as she ran toward them. Joseph was setting up some hurdles for them to practice jumping, while Jessica was clearing the junk off of the running track. "We're almost done. Did you bring your stopwatch?"

"Yes, got it right here," said Jackie as she showed them her stopwatch.

They took turns running the different courses they had set up and were having so much fun that they forgot to watch the time. It started getting dark, and they decided to meet every day until the big race. Each day, they got a little bit better and a little bit faster. This practice was really paying off, and Jackie was sure she would win her race.

It was Friday, the day before the big race, and Jackie was excited to get to the field and practice with Joseph and Jessica. However, when she got home, she had a lot of homework. It was nearly four o'clock when she was done, and she was going to be late for her last day of practice.

"Mom, it's really late, can I go to the field? It's my last day to practice before the big race. Please, can I go now?" begged Jackie

"Well, it is the weekend. I guess I can make an exception and check your homework later. I know it's late, but make sure you look both ways before crossing the streets," her mom said.

"I will," Jackie said as she dashed out the front door. There were three big streets that Jackie had to cross on the way to the field. She waited at the red light for what seemed like forever, even though no cars came. It was almost four thirty, and Jackie was afraid that Joseph and Jessica might leave thinking she wasn't coming. So at the next street, Jackie gave it half a look and went racing across the street. She was very lucky there were no cars on the road. She was not so lucky at the next street.

Jackie got so excited, only one more street until the practice fields. She put her head down and ran even faster. While Jackie could run faster with her head down, she quickly learned that she couldn't see very well. But by the time she picked her head up it was too late.

Ms. Ann, the kindly old Ape who sold the most delicious apples, came around the corner pushing her apple cart.

Jackie picked her head up just in time to see Ms. Ann, but unfortunately, she was going too fast and there was nothing she could do about it. Jackie shouted, "look out" as she closed her eyes and tried to curl into a ball.

Fortunately, Ms. Ann heard the warning and moved out of the way just before Jackie crashed full speed into the apple cart. Apples went flying everywhere, some rolled into the street and were smashed by passing trucks. Most apples just rolled through the water puddle and then the dirt ruining them.

Jackie felt horrible. She helped Ms. Ann get back onto her feet and then set about gathering all the ruined apples and stood her cart up for her. Jackie apologized several times, but all Ms. Ann would say is, "It's okay dear."

The more she said it, the worse Jackie felt. She knew how hard it was for Ms. Ann to fill up her cart with delicious apples.

Jackie felt so bad about what she had done that she decided she needed to fix it.

The next day Jackie fixed it. Instead of going to the races she had been practicing so hard for, she set off bright and early for the apple orchards. Jackie picked enough apples to overflow Ms. Ann's cart. Ms. Ann was so pleased that she insisted Jackie take a bag of apples home to her family.

Jackie thanked her, smiled, and headed home with her bag of apples. Along the way Jackie thought about the last two days. She felt sorry for running into Ms. Ann and never wanted that to happen again. Now that Jackie always looks where she is going, she is a lot safer and a lot happier.

41

Katie the Kangaroo

Katie kept everything. She never threw anything away. Katie would bring home a feather she found or a seashell from the beach. It didn't matter what it was; Katie just had to keep it. When she was little, her mom and dad thought it was cute, but as she grew older, it became a problem.

Her room was littered with toys and knick-knacks that she had collected over the years. Most things found their way into Katie's room, but she kept her prized possessions in her pouch. Since she never threw anything away, each year, things got a little worse.

Her mom, Kelly, tried to get her to clean out some of her old junk, but Katie just couldn't do it. All of her things were just too important to throw away. Katie cried every time she thought about getting rid of anything. It was like giving away a part of her life, and she just couldn't do it.

This went on for some time. Her room was becoming full, but not nearly as full as her pouch. In fact, Katie's pouch was so full that she couldn't run anymore. While the other kids were outside, running around having fun, playing games, Katie stayed inside all by herself. She would sit by the living room window for hours, watching her friends play.

Kelly just couldn't stand to see her daughter so sad. She knew something was wrong and sat Katie down for a little talk. "Katie, it breaks my heart to see you so sad," said Kelly. "Every day, you sit by the window and watch your friends play. Why won't you go out and play with them? Did you have a fight or something?"

"No, it's nothing like that, Mom. It's just hard for me to run around because my pouch is so heavy. I really miss my friends, but I just can't get rid of my precious things," said Katie as tears fell from her eyes.

"It's going to be okay, Katie, I promise. I know just what to do. Now, come with me," said Kelly as she took her hand and walked to Katie's room.

"Katie, it's time to get rid of some of your old toys. I know these things help remind you of the good times you've had, but it's the memories that are important, not the items. Here, look at this baby doll's dress. It's full of holes and stains everywhere. It's time to get rid of things like this."

"But, Mom, if I do that, I will forget about them. How will I remember them if I get rid of them?" asked Katie.

"Just wait and you'll see. First, any doll or toys that are broken or falling apart goes on your bed," Kelly said.

For the next hour, they went around Katie's room, picking up old dolls and broken toys and placing them on the bed. Katie was arranging the dolls neatly on the bed when her mom said, "Keep working, and I'll be right back." She walked out the door.

Katie spent the next few minutes making sure that the dolls were arranged perfectly. When she was done, Katie called to her mom, "I'm done, but I don't see how this is going to help."

"I'll show you," her mom said, walking into the room with her hands behind her back. "I know a way that you'll always be able to remember your dolls and stuff. With this," her mom said as she pulled out the camera from behind her back. "We can take a picture of everything before we throw anything away. Then we can put the pictures in albums, and you'll be able to remember them forever."

"Mom, that's a great idea!" said Katie as she hugged her. They spent the rest of the day going through Katie's room, taking pictures, and getting rid of the broken things and stuff she never played with. Katie got rid of so much stuff that she had a whole shelf for her most precious things. One by one, she carefully pulled them out of her pouch and gently placed them on the shelf by her bed. Now she could look at them before going to bed and when she first woke up.

Katie loves having all those pictures to remind her of all her toys. Without all that stuff in her pouch, Katie feels much better. She is able to run and play with her friends again. Katie soon realized that being with her friends makes her a lot happier than a pouch full of toys ever did.

Lenore the Ladybug

Lenore the ladybug was daydreaming in class again. Like all larvae, she dreamed of having the most beautiful ladybug wings ever. Lenore giggled every time she heard the word larva. What a silly name for a baby ladybug. The only thing sillier is this class. I've only got 7 days to get ready before my big sleep and then I get my wings. Time is running out. How is this class going to help me have the most beautiful wings ever, Lenore wondered when she heard...

"Lenore, stop your daydreaming and pay attention," said her teacher Miss Linda, "It is very important that you learn the ladybug way!"

"Sorry Miss Linda," said Lenore, but it didn't sound like she meant it.

"Now class repeat after me," Miss Linda continued, "A ladybug is always kind and sweet and we love to help everyone we meet." Those were the last words Lenore heard until the bell rang and class ended.

How silly, thought Lenore, if I help everyone I meet, then by the end of the day I'll be all sweaty and dirty. That will never help me get the most beautiful ladybug wings ever. The ladybug way sounded nice, but Lenore dreamed of beautiful wings and decided to try another way. A secret way. Yesterday in an old box labeled treasures, Lenore found a note with the words, "The Secret to Beautiful Wings" written across the top. It said to do some pretty silly things, but Lenore wanted beautiful wings, so she decided to do everything on the list.

Lenore was so focused on her "secret way" that sometimes she wasn't very nice to others. They would say hi as she went by, and Lenore would mumble things like, "No time, gotta go." She wasn't trying to be mean, she just cared more about herself and having beautiful wings. For the next seven days Lenore did all the silly things "The Secret to Beautiful wings" note said to do. It was time for Lenore's big rest, and she went to sleep positive she would wake up with beautiful wings.

Lenore woke from her big rest, and something felt different, my wings, they're finally here. She flew to the mirror expecting to see the most beautiful wings ever. However, that is not what the reflection in the mirror looked like. Her wings were red with black spots but not beautiful and shiny but dull and terrible. There must be some mistake, Lenore thought. How can this be? I did everything the note said.

Lenore started to panic when she remembered her Aunt Lucy. Her wings were so beautiful that people called her Lucy the Lovely. She will know how to fix this, so Lenore raced to Aunt Lucy's house.

Aunt Lucy listened quietly as Lenore showed her the note she found, and how she did everything on the list. She put stinky mud on her face, smelly onions on her feet and a tomato on her back for a week.

"I see the problem," said Aunt Lucy, trying not to laugh. After all Lenore had been through Aunt Lucy didn't have the heart to tell her the note wasn't real. It was a silly joke her uncle Leo played on Lenore's mom when she was a little larva. Lucy couldn't tell Lenore the Adult ladybug secret, she had to learn that on her own. Then Lucy thought of a great idea how to get Lenore back to the Ladybug way.

Lucy told Lenore about the Ladybug Game. "It's simple you get one point for every nice thing you do for someone else and you minus one point every time someone does something nice for you. No questions on how this works but when you get a score of 7 or higher for 7 days in a row, then I promise things will be better."

The first few days were really hard, and Lenore was lucky to get any points at all, but she wasn't going to give up. Every morning, Lenore thought to herself, "What can I do to get a point?"

Pretty soon, Lenore got the hang of it. She walked around all day long, looking for something nice to do for others. Now that she was thinking about it, she found lots of ways to help. What Lenore didn't expect was the warm fuzzy feeling she felt deep inside every time she helped someone. Each time she did something nice that warm feeling grew bigger, and it felt wonderful.

After just two weeks Lenore told Aunt Lucy, "The ladybug game is great, and I get at least a ten every day and once I almost got a twenty. Is it okay if I don't care about beautiful wings anymore? Helping people makes me way happier than beautiful wings ever could."

Aunt Lucy smiled, "Finally, you understand the ladybug way. A ladybug is kind and sweet and we love to help everyone we met."

As soon as Lenore figured out the Adult Ladybug secret, that true beauty comes from the inside, it happened. The goodness in her heart burst through, making her dull wings beautiful. Lenore followed the ladybug way, and her goodness grew so bright that everyone thought of her as the most beautiful ladybug ever.

Manny the Monkey

Manny was a wild monkey. He lived with his family up in the treetops with the other wild monkeys. He loved living up there. The air was always fresh and clean. On a clear day, you could see for miles. It was a great life being a wild monkey, especially when you're ten years old. You're not responsible for very much, and Manny spent most days playing with his friends, swinging in the trees, and making up cool tricks. Every now and then, he had some chores to do; but all in all, it was a pretty good life.

Most monkeys, especially ten year olds, have lots of energy, and Manny was no exception. In fact, he had more energy than most. Manny was always bouncing around. He just couldn't sit still. He had to be doing something all the time. Unfortunately, his favorite thing to do was goof off. Manny loved clowning around. He was constantly making jokes and doing crazy tricks. His clowning around often got him into trouble, but he didn't care. Manny never learned when to be serious and when it was okay to be silly.

One day, Manny was helping his mom carry the family dinner up the tree. She warned him to be careful, but Manny didn't listen. He was having too much fun jumping from branch to branch, showing off his one-handed swings. When Manny reached the top of the trees, he slipped trying to do a backflip onto the big branch. He lost his grip on the bananas and they fell to the ground. The bananas landed so hard that they spattered all over the forest floor. Manny got into big trouble for ruining the family's dinner. While Manny felt bad about ruining dinner, he didn't learn the lesson that there was a time to be serious and a time to be silly. For Manny, any time was a good time for being silly. He thought his parents were too strict and were always spoiling his fun.

"One of these days, Manny, your fooling around is going to get you into real trouble," his mom said. Unfortunately, Manny didn't really listen and thought his mom was just trying to ruin all his fun.

Several months later, it was the rainy season, and there was a huge rainstorm. It rained for two weeks straight, and the grown-ups became concerned. If it didn't stop raining soon, the river would overflow, and that could wash away the trees they lived in. Two nights later, the worst thing imaginable happened. The river overflowed and started rushing towards their trees. The trees were strong and stood for a while, but the water was stronger, and one by one, the trees began to fall.

Manny's dad came swinging in, shouting, "It's time to go, the river is coming and we need to get to higher ground where it will be safe. I will lead the way. Maggie, I want you to hold your mother's hand, and Manny, you follow behind them." Looking right at Manny, his dad said, "This is serious, I don't want any of your goofing off. The branches are slippery, so hold on tight with both hands. If we all stay together, everything will be all right. Okay, let's go. Everyone stay close and follow me."

Manny's dad led them through the rain and wind. When they looked down, they could see the water was still rising. With the branches being wet and slippery, Manny's dad was worried that if they didn't hold on tight, they could fall into the water and be swept away. After what seemed like forever, the rain stopped, but the branches were still wet and very slippery. They had traveled a long way and took a short break before they went the rest of the way.

When they started up again, Manny was still in the back and began to get a little bored. He had been this way many times, and he started to become less careful. At first, he just stopped, holding on extra tight. Then Manny started doing his one-handed swings, and that's when it happened. The branch was soaking wet, Manny's hand slipped off, and he screamed. Manny began to fall, heading straight towards the river. He realized that he was going to land in the river and there was nothing he could do to stop himself.

Just as Manny was about to hit the water, his dad grabbed him by the arm and pulled him back into the tree. Manny couldn't believe it; his dad had saved him from being carried away by the river!

At that moment, Manny realized just how foolish he had been. He could have been swept away forever because of his goofing off. Manny was shaking and he couldn't talk until he was safely back in the treetops with his family.

"I'm so sorry," Manny said. "I never thought anything bad could happen. When you said stop goofing off, I thought you were being too strict and you didn't want me to have any fun. Now I know that you weren't trying to stop my fun. You were trying to protect me. I promise I will never ever goof off again. I will be serious all the time."

"Now, Manny," his dad said, "we are not happy about what just happened, but we are very happy that you are all right. While now was not the time to goof off, we are not saying you have to be serious all the time either. In fact, it's important that you have time to fool around with your friends. You need to realize that there are other times when you need to be serious, like now. I think you may have just learned that lesson."

His dad was right; he did finally learn his lesson. Manny hardly ever gets in trouble because he knows when not to goof off. Manny is a lot happier and a lot safer, because he has learned that there is a time to be serious and a time to have fun.

Nancy the Nightingale

Nancy had a beautiful voice. When she sang, all the other birds would stop to listen. She always dreamed of being a famous singer. When she was little, she would pretend that she was one of the Boppin' Birds. They were the most famous singing group in the world. The Boppin' Birds were Nancy's favorite group.

One day, her music teacher, Mrs. Bell, said, "Listen up, class. I have a very special announcement to make. Yesterday, I spoke with my good friend, Sarah the swan, the leader of the Boppin' Birds. Sarah told me that later this year, Betty the Blue Jay will be retiring, and they are looking for someone to replace her. I told Sarah there are a lot of talented singers here and sent her some tapes to listen to. She liked them so much that the Boppin' Birds are coming here. Anyone interested in trying out for the Boppin' Birds can see me after school. Who knows? Maybe one of you could be the next star."

Nancy couldn't believe her ears. The Boppin' Birds were coming here. She just had to meet them. When school ended, she ran straight to Mrs. Bell's office.

"Hello, Nancy, come in," said Mrs. Bell. "I guess you want a tryout sheet."

"Oh, no, Mrs. Bell," said Nancy as she let out a little laugh. "I'm not good enough to sing with them. I was just hoping that since you're such good friends with Sarah that maybe I could meet them."

"Are you kidding, Nancy? Not good enough? You have a voice like an angel!" said Mrs. Bell. "You would be perfect for the Boppin' Birds. You're my most talented singer."

"I'm not a bad singer, but I don't believe that I'm good enough to be a real singer. I'm definitely not good enough for the Boppin' Birds," said Nancy.

"But Nancy," said Mrs. Bell, "for as long as I've known you, all you have ever talked about was being a Boppin' Bird someday."

"That's just a silly dream, Mrs. Bell," said Nancy. "I really don't think I'm good enough to sing with the Boppin' Birds. They are the best singers in the whole world, and I'm just plain old Nancy."

"Not good enough?" said Mrs. Bell. "Well, I think you're good enough. You have a beautiful voice and you're the hardest worker in my class. I'll let you in on a little secret. When Sarah was a little girl, she was no different than you. She had a beautiful voice and practiced every day, but she was afraid to sing in front of people. She was worried that she was not good enough and they would laugh at her."

"No way," said Nancy, "I don't believe it. Sarah afraid? How could she be afraid? She has the best voice in the world! Are you joking with me?"

"No, it's all true," said Sarah as she walked into the room.

"Oh, my gosh! You're Sarah!" shouted Nancy. "You're my favorite singer! I can't believe you're here!"

"Well, believe it, Nancy. And you can believe what Mrs. Bell said. When I was little, I was so scared. I wasn't a superstar. I was just a plain old swan. That's when Mrs. Bell told me all I had to do was to believe in myself. She said to never give up on my dreams. I had the talent and worked really hard. The only thing I needed to do was believe. So I took her advice, gathered up all my courage, and went on stage and sang. The audience seemed to really like it and asked for more songs. Ever since that night, I've believed in myself. Now look at me—I'm the lead singer for the Boppin' Birds! From the tapes that Mrs. Bell sent me, it sounds like you could do the same."

"Do you really believe I can do it?" Nancy asked shyly.

"Yes, I do, but it doesn't matter what I believe. It matters what you believe. I hope I see you at tryouts on Saturday," said Sarah, and she left for her rehearsal.

Nancy went home and thought about what they had said. She did have a good voice and worked hard. If they believed, maybe she should believe in herself.

The night of tryouts, Nancy was very nervous. The other singers were really good, and she started to doubt herself. That's when she remembered what Sarah and Mrs. Bell said—"Just believe in yourself." So Nancy gathered up her courage, went out on stage, and sang. When the song ended, the entire audience stood up and clapped for over ten minutes. When the last singers were done, Sarah took the stage to announce the winner.

"We had a lot of great singers tonight," said Sarah, "and I think we have found our next group member. I am pleased to say that when Betty retires later this year, Nancy will be taking her place."

Nancy was so excited to hear her name called! This was the best day of her life. She was going to be a Boppin' Bird! Nancy was so happy her dream was coming true, and it's all because she worked hard and believed in herself.

Oscar the Owl

Oscar the owl lived in a big oak tree in the back of the forest. He was very smart and knew lots of great stories. Every Friday morning all the little birds gathered around his tree. They couldn't wait to hear what story Oscar was going to tell.

Pete the parakeet and Brian the blue jay were best friends and they also lived in the forest. Each day they would get together and play games like tag and hide and go seek. However, their favorite thing to do was to listen to the great stories that Oscar would tell.

Sometimes he would tell stories about pirates or princesses. Some days, the stories were about frogs or bears. No matter what the stories were about, they were always great.

"Hey, Oscar, what story are you going to tell us today?" asked Pete.

"Well," said Oscar, "what kind of story would you like to hear? Would you like to hear about strange faraway places? Or would you prefer an adventure story? Perhaps you would enjoy a nice tale about a magician who lived long ago."

It didn't take the kids long to decide, and they started chanting, "Magician, magician, magician!"

"Magician it is," said Oscar. The kids immediately became silent as they didn't want to miss one word of the story. "Once upon a time, there lived a magician named Merlin," Oscar began. He told them of Merlin and all the wonderful things he had done. The kids loved the story, and when Oscar was done, they cheered and yelled for more. "That was great, Oscar, tell us another story, please," begged the kids.

"Not today," said Oscar. "I'm glad you enjoyed the story, but you know the rule—only one story. Goodbye, everyone, I'll see you all next week."

One by one, they thanked Oscar and flew off until only Pete and Brian remained.

"Is there something I can do for you?" Oscar asked them.

"We just wanted to tell you how much we like your stories," said Brian.

"Yeah, it was great," said Pete. "I've been coming every Friday forever, and each week, you make up a new awesome story. How do you do it?"

"Oh, I don't make them up," said Oscar. "Every story I tell comes from one of the books in the Great Library. It has thousands of books filled with stories."

"Wow, the library must be an awesome place. I wish I could go there," said Brian.

"I don't see why not," said Oscar. "I'm on my way there now. You can come with me if it's okay with your parents. Go ask them and I'll wait right here for you."

Pete and Brian flew home as fast as they could. "Mom, Oscar is going to the Great Library, and he said we could go with him if it is all right with you. Please can we go?" begged Pete and Brian.

"As long as you two stay together and use your good manners, it should be okay. Now behave yourselves and listen to Oscar. When you're done, come straight home," said their mothers.

The boys thanked their moms and raced back to Oscar. The three of them headed off to the great library. When they arrived, Pete and Brian opened the front door and just stood there. They had never seen so many books before. There were books about dinosaurs and horses and others had pictures of dolphins and great white sharks. The only problem was that Pete and Brian didn't know how to read.

"No problem," said Oscar, "I can teach you to read so you can enjoy all these wonderful books."

Pete and Brian were good students and did all the lessons that Oscar gave them. They worked very hard, and before they knew it, they could read. Now that they can read, Pete and Brian spend most days in the Great Library. They don't have to wait until Fridays to hear a great story. They learned that the best part about reading is that any time you want to hear a story, all you have to do is pick up a book and read one.

Paul the Panther

Paul the panther was having a perfectly wonderful day exploring the mountain until he saw them. It was Peter, the local panther bully, and his little group of friends and they loved picking on him.

"Hey everybody, look it's Paul. Are you lost or something?" asked Peter. "This side of the mountain is for big kids only, no babies allowed. Why don't you go back to the baby side before you get hurt?" teased Peter as he jumped from the ledge and walked towards Paul.

"I'm not a baby, I can play on this side of the mountain if I want to," said Paul in his bravest voice.

"Oh, really?" asked Peter. "Think you're a big kid now? Think you're brave and all that? Well, I still think you're nothing but a tiny little baby. You're not a real panther, just a little baby putty-tat."

The other panthers laughed and joined in, "Little baby putty-tat, little baby putty-tat…"

"Stop it!" shouted Penny, a slightly older panther and Paul's best friend. "He's only one year younger than you. Can't you big grown-up panthers think of anything better to do than pick on Paul?"

"Yeah, I can think of something," said Peter with a smirk on his face. "Come on, follow me." Peter turned, ran up the path and the other panthers chased after him. Penny knew exactly where they were going. That path led straight to Stink Pass. They were going to try to make Paul jump across it.

"No, Paul, don't go," said Penny. "They're going to make fun of you and try to get you to do something dumb. Please don't do it. It's not worth it."

"Penny, you don't understand," said Paul. "They've teased me all my life. If I don't stand up for myself and prove I'm brave, they'll never stop teasing me. This is my one chance to show them I'm not a little baby. I'm sorry, Penny, I have to do this," said Paul and he raced after them.

"Well, I'm not going to watch you make a fool of yourself," yelled Penny. But Paul was long gone and didn't hear a word she said. Penny stood there all alone, thinking to herself. "Nope, not going there, that path goes to Stink Pass. It was a shortcut through the swamp, but no one used it. The swamp and its bubbles were nasty! When she was young, a swamp bubble burst all over her cousin Pedro when he tried to cross. Her Aunt Peggy wouldn't let him into the house for a week. Deep down Penny knew no matter how bad it smelled, Paul was her best friend and she needed to help and leapt after him.

Paul finally caught up to the other panthers at the edge of the swamp. They were all standing on the big ledge known as Stink Pass. Even from here it smelled terrible, and Paul's eyes started to water.

"So, Paul, still think you're brave enough to hang out with us?" asked Peter. "Then prove it. I dare you to jump across Stink Pass."

Paul walked up to the edge of Stink Pass. The closer he got the worse it smelled, and his eyes watered so badly that he could barely see.

"It was only eight feet across," thought Paul, "That's nothing, he could easily jump twice that far. But with his watery eyes, what if he jumped too late and his paw hit the swamp? He would fall in, and they would tease him for the rest of his life. After another minute of thinking, Paul finally said, "I'm not jumping across Stink Pass, it doesn't prove anything."

"It proves you're a scaredy cat and not a real panther." said Peter.

"Watch, I'll show you who's a real panther." He turned and leapt across Stink Pass. Peter landed safely on the other side, turned, and began teasing Paul again, "scaredy cat, scaredy cat," and the others joined in until Paul couldn't take it anymore.

He was about to say I'll do it when he heard Penny's voice shouting, "No Paul, don't do it! It's not right and you know better!"

"But Penny, I have to prove that I'm brave, so they will stop teasing me," he said a little frustrated that Penny didn't understand. But Penny, being two years older, did understand. She understood better than anyone and moved between Paul and the others.

"I see," said Penny. "You're brave enough, or should I say foolish enough to jump over Stink Pass, but you're not brave enough to stand up to your "supposed friends" and do the right thing."

At that moment, Paul finally realized that being brave didn't have anything to do with taking dares or impressing other people. Doing dares was easy, but it takes real courage to stand up for yourself and do the right thing

"I'm sorry Penny, you're right," said Paul. "I'm not jumping across Stink Pass, and I'm done trying to impress you, Peter. Come on Penny let's go." Paul turned and walked away. The other panthers saw how silly Peter looked standing on the wrong side of the swamp and wondered why they ever followed him. Then one by one they turned and headed home.

From that day on, Paul was known as the bravest panther around, not because he did crazy dares, but because he always found the courage to do the right thing. Paul found his true courage when he was brave enough to stop doing dares to impress others and that made him truly happy.

Quincy the Quail

Quincy was a shy little bird. He lived in a beautiful brown nest near the top of a red berry bush. A little stream flowed underneath his bush, so Quincy always had plenty of fresh water to drink and berries to eat. The best part about his home was that it was located right in the middle of the park.

Each day after lunch, Quincy would climb to the top of his bush and watch the other kids playing in the park. Sometimes he watched Artie and the squirrels play baseball. Artie was a great pitcher, and the squirrels won a lot of games. They were his favorite team to watch because they always looked like they were having fun, even when they didn't win.

Right in front of Quincy's bush were the basketball courts. Quincy loved basketball; it was his favorite game to play. Quincy would sneak out late at night and play basketball by himself for hours and hours. You see, Quincy was very shy and not very good at making friends. He was so afraid to talk to the other kids that poor Quincy never had a friend to play with.

One day, Quincy was sitting on top of his bush watching Betty the bunny and Sally the squirrel play basketball. They really weren't very good at it, but they seemed to be having a lot of fun anyway. It was Sally's turn to shoot. She threw the ball as hard as she could. It bounced off the backboard, went flying off the court, and rolled until it stopped right in front of Quincy's bush.

When Sally picked up the ball, she noticed Quincy sitting on the top of the bush. "Oh, hello," said Sally, "I didn't see you there. My name is Sally. What's your name?"

"My name is Quincy," he answered shyly.

"Nice to meet you, Quincy. What are you doing sitting here all by yourself?" asked Sally. "It's a beautiful day. You should be playing with your friends, not sitting here all alone."

"I would like that very much, but I'm really shy and don't have any friends to play with," said Quincy.

That's so sad, thought Sally. "You shouldn't be afraid to talk to people," she said. "What's the worst thing that could happen? They don't like you and you're still alone, so no difference. But what if they do like you? Then you'll have friends to play with. Why don't you come play basketball with me and my friend, Betty?" asked Sally. "We're not very good, but we're having a lot of fun."

"Do you mean it?" asked Quincy. "I would like that very much."

"Sure, come on," said Sally, "I'll introduce you to my friend Betty."

Quincy and Sally walked back to the basketball court, and Sally introduced Quincy to Betty.

"Hey, Betty," said Sally, "this is Quincy. He doesn't have a lot of friends, so I told him he could play basketball with us. I hope that's okay with you?"

"Are you kidding? Making new friends is my favorite thing to do," said Betty. "Hello, Quincy, I'm Betty. It's nice to meet you. I hope you'll be our new friend. Although, I'm not sure you will want to be after you see how bad I am at basketball."

"Well, to tell the truth, I've been watching you two, and you're not that bad," said Quincy. "You just need someone to show you the right way to hold the basketball. Here, I'll show you. All you have to do is put your two hands like this and shoot."

Quincy showed them the right way to stand, and after a little practice, Betty and Sally were making all kinds of baskets. They had a great time playing basketball with their new friend, Quincy.

"You know, Quincy, basketball is a lot more fun when you can make a basket. I'm really glad we met you," said Sally.

"Yeah, thanks for teaching us how to shoot. I had a lot of fun today. I hope we can be friends and play again," said Betty.

"I really like playing with both of you. I hope we can do it again real soon," said Quincy.

Betty and Sally introduced Quincy to some of the other kids. After a little while, Quincy learned not to be so shy. Now he has lots of new fiends because he is no longer afraid to talk to people, and that makes him very happy.

Ronnie the Raccoon

Ronnie let out a big yawn as he sat up in bed and stretched his arms high above his head. The sunlight peeking through his window was calling his name. He hopped out of bed, ran to the window, and looked out upon the most perfect day. Best of all, it was the last week of summer vacation and his mom said he could do whatever he wanted.

Ronnie threw his cleats over his shoulder and walked into the kitchen where his mom was making breakfast for the family. "Hi Mom," he said, "I'm going to Cousin Rickey's house."

"Breakfast first!" She said in her most serious mom voice.

One look at his mom and Ronnie knew better than to argue with her. Ronnie gobbled up his breakfast, put his plate in the sink, kissed his mom on the cheek and took off for Rickey's house.

As Ronnie ran up to Rickey's house his Aunt Rena was standing in the doorway with a big smile on her face and asked, "running a little late today?" as she opened the screen door.

"Really late, my mom made me eat breakfast," said Ronnie.

"Oh, how terrible, Rickey is in the kitchen with the same problem," said Aunt Rena as she stepped aside to let Ronnie go by.

Rickey was putting his plate in the sink when Ronnie came running into the kitchen all excited asking "Are you ready?"

"Oh yeah!" said Rickey. "The soccer equipment is all packed up and ready to go. I'll go get our soccer team friends; you go get our school friends, and we'll meet at the big field in one hour"

One hour, I'm going to need some help thought Ronnie. He knew what to do and ran as fast as he could to get Zachy the Zebra's help. They gathered their school friends so quickly that they arrived at the field early and started clearing off the branches. They had just finished when Rickey arrived. They quickly picked teams and the games began.

They were having so much fun that they forgot to take water breaks. In fact, they completely forgot to bring water and after several games they all desperately needed a drink of water.

"Why don't we go to the red barn," said Zachy, "The hose in the back has the coldest most delicious water I've ever tasted."

Ronnie said, "Follow me, I know a short cut to the red barn"

They talked and laughed about what fun they had playing soccer the whole way to the barn. When they arrived, Zachy showed them the hose that had the coldest, most delicious water. Yakkie the yak drank first since she was the hottest. The rest of the kids got in line and waited to take their turn. Ronnie needed to sit down more than he needed a drink. He pulled up one of the wooden crates and plopped down hard. Ronnie landed so hard that the crate smashed and out came a bag of round purple discs that looked like candies.

"Jackpot!" Ronnie said excitedly as he held the bag up for all to see. Then he reached into the bag and was about to eat some when Zachy shouted, "No don't eat that! You have no idea what it is."

"Looks like candy," said Ronnie, then he sniffed, "smells like candy," he put his tongue on one, "tastes like candy, so it must be candy."

Everyone yelled, "No!" but it was too late, Ronnie threw a handful into his mouth and Rickey became extremely nervous.

"Don't worry, I'm fine," Ronnie started to say when purple spots started popping out all over his face, "Umm, I don't feel so good."

Rickey helped Ronnie get on Zachy's back and they raced him home as fast as they could. They put Ronnie in his bed while his mom called Dr. Alana the Alpaca.

All of Ronnie's friends nervously waited outside his room while the doctor was in there. Finally, Dr. Alana opened the door and with a smile on her face said, "come on in, your friend's fine, this time,"

Dr. Alana explained that those pills were made for sick horses and not candies for kids. She told them that Ronnie was really lucky, and it could have been much worse. She made all the kids promise not to eat or touch anything that they did not know what it was.

If you're not sure what something is, then ask an adult you trust before eating it. All the kids promised never to touch or eat anything they did not know what it was.

From then on, all the kids kept their promise and never ate or even touched anything that they did not know what it was. Ronnie was especially happy because he followed Dr. Alana's rule, and he never had a problem again.

Sid the Squirrel

Sid the Squirrel pedaled his bike as fast as he could. He was so excited, the first day back to school after summer vacation was the best. You get to see all your friends again and hear about all the cool things they did over the summer. When Sid arrived, Sam the Squirrel was telling everyone about the new kid on his baseball team, Artie the Aardvark.

"I've never seen anyone pitch so fast," said Sam. "Artie's super nice and such a good pitcher that we won first place."

"That's nothing," said Sid, "before we moved here, my team won the State Championship, but I don't like to brag."

Yeah right, thought Sam, all Sid does is brag. Sam liked Sid a lot, but sometimes he wished Sid didn't tell so many unbelievable stories.

Sally the Squirrel was so excited, "Guess what I did over the summer? We went to Carnival Corner. It's amazing and super huge! My family went twice this summer. Both times we stayed all day and still didn't see everything. There's an adult section, but you have to be 16 or older to get in."

Molly the Mongoose excitedly said, "I didn't know they opened Carnival Corner. I've been wanting to go ever since they started building it!"

"Me too!" said Heidi the Hyena. "I can't wait to see what's inside."

"I know everything about Carnival Corner," said Sid. "Bet you didn't know that my Uncle Santiago practically built Carnival Corner."

"No way!" the kids shouted as they looked at Sid waiting to hear more.

Sid continued, "It's true, he was project manager and I got to see it being built. I'll never forget the first time my uncle took me to the adult section. Amazing! I wanted to tell you about it, but Uncle Santiago made me promise not to tell anyone.

"What's in the adult section?" Sam asked, not sure if this was true or one of Sid's stories.

The other kids began shouting, "Tell us, tell us."

"Okay, okay," said Sid quieting them down and continued telling his story. "You know the small tight rope they have by the front entrance? It's like six inches off the ground. Well, in the adult section it's ten feet off the ground, with no net."

"That sounds terrifying," said Heidi, "No way I'm doing that."

"I did it on my first try," said Sid.

"That's amazing," said Molly.

Sid shrugged his shoulder saying, "no big deal, but the best thing in the adult section, is Barrel Jumping. So cool, you ride a bike really fast down a dirt path and up a ramp. Then you go flying over the barrels and land on the ramp on the other side. It's so dangerous that you have to be 18 or older to try and sign some papers about getting hurt. It took me a few tries but after thirty days in a row, I got really good at it..."

Sid was about to continue telling his story when the school bell rang, they went inside, and all agreed to meet at the park after school.

When they all arrived at the park, Sam asked Sid to tell them more about barrel jumping. He wasn't sure if he believed Sid, but it sounded so exciting, he just had to hear more about it.

Sid was about to start bragging about barrel jumping when Jackie the Jaguar said, "Sid, didn't you hear. They built a bike ramp right here in the park! No barrels, but you can show us all how good you are."

"I can't wait to learn how to jump," said Sam. They all hopped on their bikes and followed Jackie to the new bike ramp.

Sid took one look at the bike ramp and became very scared. While it was true that Sid's uncle was project manager of Carnival Corner and did show him the adult section, but Sid never did barrel jumping. His Uncle said it was too big, too dangerous, and Sid was not old enough.

For one second Sid thought about doing the bike ramp but knew if he tried, he would get hurt. Sid regretted making up the barrel jumping story. In fact, he regretted all the stories he made up. Just then he heard all the kids shouting, "Come on Sid, show us how it's done!"

Sid knew there was only one thing to do, tell the truth. He was scared because he didn't know how the other kids would react, but he knew telling the truth was the right thing to do. Sid took a deep breath and told all his friends that he really didn't know how to barrel jump. He made the whole thing up. Sid told them when he was small, other kids talked about the cool things they did, and he didn't do anything cool, so he made up a story to fit in. Sid lowered his head as a few tears ran down his face and he told everyone he was sorry for making up stories. He would understand if they didn't want to be friends anymore.

Sam put his arm around Sid and said, "we don't like you because of the stories you tell, we like you because you are a good person."

"That's right" said the other kids and they all told Sid why they liked him. None of the reasons had anything to do with the stories he made up. Sid realized he didn't need to tell stories for people to like him, he just needed to be himself. From then on, Sid only told the truth, and he was a lot happier because of it.

Timmy the Turtle

Timmy just had to win. Ever since he was a little boy, he dreamed of being a famous artist. Now his big chance was finally here.

The winner of next week's contest got to work with Mr. Teddy, the world famous statue maker. Mr. Teddy was his hero, and Timmy just had to win.

Timmy, along with twenty other students, walked into the classroom bright and early Monday morning. Mr. Teddy was standing at the front of the class, and when everyone took their seats, he said, "Good morning, everyone. My name is Mr. Teddy. Welcome to our statue contest. I know you're all anxious, so let's get right to it. The contest is simple. Underneath this cloth is a statue, and all you have to do is make your statue look exactly like mine. The student whose statue looks the closest to mine will be the winner. You only get one chance, so take your time and do it right. Remember, this is not a race. It's about how well you can make your statue look like mine. You have all day to finish. Now, before we begin, are there any questions?"

Everyone was too excited to get started and could not think of any questions.

"Well, if there are no questions, I would like to give you some advice before you begin. Today you will be making your statues out of coral. Now I know most of you have never worked with coral before, so let me warn you, coral is very brittle and falls apart very easily. Take your time, be careful, do it right, and you should have no problem," said Mr. Teddy. He passed out a large piece of coral to everyone. "Now would you like to see what you are making today?"

Timmy was sure it was going to be something really hard to make. He was so surprised when Mr. Teddy pulled off the cloth and underneath it was a simple flower. A simple flower? What kind of test is this? thought everyone.

We can make flowers in our sleep. It must be a trick, thought Timmy. The class soon learned that this simple flower was a lot harder than it looked.

"Now remember, this is not a race. You have all day, so take your time and do it right. Good luck to everyone. You may now begin," said Mr. Teddy as he walked to the back of the class and sat down.

This is going to be so easy, thought most of the class. They all wanted to be the first one done to prove how good they were. They soon learned that trying to be the first one done was a big mistake. Mr. Teddy gave them a pretty big piece of coral, and they needed to carve a lot off of the sides. Now the quick way that many people tried was to cut off a big chunk all at once. However, the right way to do this was to take a little off at a time and slowly make your way to the middle.

Trent was the first one to begin. He quickly drew his lines on the coral and tried to cut off a big piece all at once. As soon as he made his first cut, the coral crumbled and fell apart. His statue was ruined and he was out of the contest. More than half the class ruined their statues the same way.

Timmy decided to listen to what Mr. Teddy said. "Take your time and do it right." He started by taking off small pieces one at a time. After the first hour, there were only eight people left. Every time someone tried to rush or take a shortcut, their statue would fall apart. Pretty soon, the contest was down to only three—Timmy, Thomas, and Terry.

Thomas wanted his statue to be perfect, but he still wanted to be first. He looked over and saw that Terry was almost done. He had to go faster. While smoothing out the stem, he went too fast and his flower split in half and he was out of the contest.

Now it was down to Terry and Timmy. They looked at each other and realized they were both very close to being done. Terry only needed to put the finishing touches on the petals and she would be done. Timmy was just about to speed up when he remembered what Mr. Teddy said. "The most important thing about making this statue is to take your time and do it right." Timmy took a deep breath, relaxed, and went back to doing it slow and right.

Terry saw that Timmy was almost finished and knew if she just went a little tiny bit faster, she could beat him. Unfortunately, that little extra speed made her hand slip and she accidently cut off the tip of one of the petals. Timmy continued to take his time and do it the right way and he finished his statue without any mistakes.

Mr. Teddy looked at both statues and said to the class, "I hope you have all learned something today. Making statues is not about going fast. It's about doing it right. You have all worked hard, but there can only be one winner. That winner is Timmy. Let's give him a big round of applause!"

Everyone cheered for Timmy. He couldn't believe it. He won. He actually won. Timmy couldn't be happier and it was all because he realized that if you want something done right, you can't take shortcuts. Timmy's lifelong dream to work with Mr. Teddy was coming true, and it was all because he took his time and did it the right way.

Uni was sad. She was almost seven years old and still didn't know what her magic power was. You see, unicorns believe that their magic power makes them special.

Her dad, Ulysses, had strong powers. He could move things with his mind.

Uni's mom, Urell, could make food grow bigger. She could make one slice of bread grow so big, it could feed the whole town. Yes, both her parents had strong powers.

That's why Uni felt so bad. Everyone thought that Uni would have a strong power too. Most unicorns figured out their power when they were four or five years old. Uni would be seven in two weeks and she still didn't know what her power was. How was she ever going to be special without a magic power?

Uni told her parents how she felt. "When will I learn what my power is? I feel like a big nothing without a power. I want to have a great power so I can be really special like you guys."

"Oh, Uni, you are very special," her mom said as she gave her a big hug. "We love you just the way you are. We don't care what your power is. You're great, and everyone thinks so."

"That's right, sweetheart, your mom and I love you very much. Having a magic power doesn't make you special. It's what you do with the talents that you do have. That's what makes you special," explained her dad. "You're very special, and I'm not just saying that because you are my daughter. It's true. I can't even think of one person who doesn't like you. Even those mean kids across the river like you.

You make everyone you meet happy. Hmm, I wonder…" her dad said with a strange look on his face.

"What is it, Ulysses? What are you thinking?" asked Urell.

"Nothing, dear, just a strange thought. Come here, Uni, give me a hug," said her dad. "I have a great idea. Why don't you come with us tomorrow? We're going to the southern village because five days ago, there was a terrible landslide. It destroyed most of their village, and we're going to bring them some food and help them rebuild their homes. They need all the help they can get, and if I'm right, they need your help most of all."

"Sure, Dad, I'd love to go and help. I'm kind of tired now, so I'm going to go to bed. Goodnight, I love you," said Uni as she hugged her parents and went off to bed. As Uni lay in her bed, she wondered about what her dad said. What did he mean they could really use my help? It didn't make any sense. She didn't have any talent that could help those poor people. Uni fell asleep, wondering how a unicorn with no magical powers was something the village really needed.

The next day, the village was worse than Uni imagined. Their homes were completely destroyed. Those poor kids lost everything. All their toys and everything they owned were buried under tons of rocks. The younger kids sat together in a circle, looking very sad. Uni had never seen anything so sad in her whole life. Uni knew she just had to do something to help them.

Uni walked over to the kids and started talking to them. She told them how lucky they were that no one got hurt during this terrible accident. Uni told them that everything was going to be all right, and even though things looked really bad now, they would get better. One by one, they slowly believed that Uni was right and things would get better.

In no time at all, they were all running around, playing games, and laughing. They had so much fun with Uni that they forgot all about their problems. When it was time to go, the kids begged Uni to stay, but it was late and she had to leave. Uni didn't want to go, but she told the kids she would be back tomorrow. All the kids gave her a big hug and thanked her for such a great day.

As they walked home, her dad said, "Uni, that was a really great thing you did today. You helped that village more than your mom and I put together."

"What are you talking about, Dad?" asked Uni. "Mom made enough food to last for days, and you cleared away a million boulders. I didn't do anything special. All I did was play with the kids."

"Are you kidding? You helped them more than you know," her dad said. "Those kids lost everything and haven't smiled in days. Their parents were starting to wonder if they would ever be happy again. Then you came along, and suddenly their kids are laughing and happy again. You know nothing makes a parent feel better than seeing their children happy. Today you took a village that lost everything and gave them hope and happiness. In your own special way, you made the lives of all those people better. Now I don't know if that counts as a magic power or not, but it certainly makes you a very special person."

Just then, Uni realized her parents were right. She didn't need a magic power to be special. What made her special was her ability to make others happy. Uni didn't know if that counted as a magic power or not, but making other people happy sure did make her feel magical.

Vinny the Vulture

Vinny was crying again. "Go see what he's whining about now," said Victor, his older brother.

"It's probably just a little scratch," said Vicky, Vinny's sister, "Will you please stop crying like a baby."

Just then, Vinny came around the corner, holding his wing and crying.

"What's the matter now, Vinny?" sighed Victor.

"Well," Vinny sobbed as he wiped his eyes dry, "we were playing over there and Vance pushed me really hard. I crashed into that big sharp rock and cut my wing. Now it's bleeding really bad." Vinny started to sob again.

Vicky took one look at Vinny's wing and saw that he had a small scratch with a little blood on it. She couldn't believe Vinny was making such a big deal out of such a little cut. Vicky had enough of Vinny's whining and said, "Knock it off, Vinny. It's only a little scratch."

"Yeah, quit it," said Victor. "Why do you have to be such a crybaby? It's really embarrassing having a crybaby for a brother. When are you going to grow up?"

"Quit it, Victor, I'm telling Mom on you!" screamed Vinny as he went home.

When Vinny got home, he called, "Mom, Mom, I got hurt really bad, and Victor and Vicky didn't believe me. They just made fun of me." Vinny started to cry again.

"Now, Vinny," his mom said, "stop that. You weren't crying when you first came in, so there is no reason for you to start crying now. Calm down, dry your eyes, and tell me what happened."

As his mom cleaned his cut and put a Band-Aid on it, Vinny told her what happened.

"Well, that wasn't very nice of your brother and sister. Later I will have a talk with them about teasing you, but right now, I want to talk to you."

"Sure, Mom, what do you want to talk about?" asked Vinny.

"We have to talk about the way you behave when you get hurt," his mom said.

"But Mom!" interrupted Vinny. "It hurt so bad. Why don't you believe me?"

"Honey, I do believe you," his mom said. "I was the same way when I was your age. It hurts so bad you think it will never stop. Most cuts and bruises hurt really bad at first, and they start to feel better after a minute or two."

"But my cuts and bruises don't feel better after a minute or two," said Vinny.

"The reason they don't feel better is because your crying makes it worse. Your body tenses up, and that makes it feel worse. When I was your age, my mom told me that if I could be tough for two minutes, it would start to feel better. I wasn't sure I believed her, but I was tired of being picked on. So I tried, and it worked. Now, go outside and think about what I said, okay?" said Vinny's mom as she hugged him and sent him on his way.

Vinny went outside, sat on the swing, and thought about what his mom had said. Vinny didn't think his mom's idea would work, but it sure would be nice if everyone stopped calling him a crybaby. Maybe he would give it a try.

About two weeks later, while Victor, Vicky, and Vinny were having flying races at the park, it happened. Vinny was trying to pass Vicky and his left wing hit the branch and he tumbled to the ground. He saw the cuts and scrapes on his wing and was about to cry when he remembered what his mom had said. "Be brave, don't cry. Be brave, don't cry."

Vicky flew down looking very concerned and asked, "Vinny, are you okay?"

Vinny thought about it for a minute and his mom was right. His wing did hurt really bad at first, but it was already starting to feel better. He couldn't believe it—crying did make it feel worse! "No, I'm okay, Vicky, it's just a few scratches," said Vinny as he wiped the dirt off. "Let's go finish the race." Vinny got up and flew away.

Vicky couldn't believe how brave Vinny was being. Normally, he would have cried and cried until they took him home and missed out on all the fun. Instead, Vinny was being brave, and they had a great day at the park. He even overheard his brother, Victor, telling one of his friends how tough Vinny was being.

Victor's words made Vinny feel good inside. Things were going to be different from now on. Vinny stopped crying about every little thing, and pretty soon, people stopped calling him a crybaby. After a while, they even started to think of Vinny as being tough. Yes, things got a lot better for Vinny when he realized that being brave for a few minutes was a lot more fun and a lot less painful than crying about every little thing.

Wally the Whale

Wally was a blue whale that lived in the ocean with his mom and dad. He didn't have any brothers or sisters, but he did have his best friend, Willy. They did everything together. They spent hours at the splash zone, practicing their splashes.

Wally and Willy went to the splash zone nearly every day. They began by swimming down really far, then come rushing up out of the water, and when they landed sideways, they made a huge splash. The whales loved to play and have contests to see who could make the biggest splash or the highest or the one that went the furthest. Wally never cared about winning; it was just fun being there with his best friend, Willy.

Things were going pretty good for Wally until one day, his parents told him that they were moving. Wally had never been anywhere else and was very upset about having to leave his friends, especially Willy. They had been best friends for as long as he could remember. What was he going to do without Willy? Wally was very mad at his parents.

Moving day finally came, and Wally said goodbye to all his friends. It was really hard to say goodbye to everyone, especially Willy. Wally was so mad that he didn't speak to his parents the whole trip to the new house. It was a long way to their new home, and after what seemed like forever, they finally arrived. The place was really nice, but Wally didn't care. He was too upset about leaving his friends. He didn't know any of the kids and he was sure that he would never have a friend like Willy again.

While Wally's mom and dad unpacked all their stuff, Wally went out to see if he could find any other kids. He swam around for a while but he didn't see any other whales. When he came back home, he was madder than when he left. He was so upset that he went straight to his room and stayed there for the rest of the day.

His mom tried to cheer him up, but Wally was too sad about leaving his friends. For the next week, Wally did nothing but complain about how he had no friends and how much he missed his old home. Finally, his mom had enough.

"Wally," she said, "I'm sorry that you miss your friend, Willy, but we had no choice and had to move here. It's been over two weeks and you've done nothing but complain about how terrible your life is. Well, it's time you stopped complaining and did something about it. Now you're coming with me."

Wally's mom took him to a place called The Hole. It was a very large and very deep swimming area where some of the older kids went to play. When they arrived, they saw a group of dolphins doing some tricks. Some did flips while others were doing spins and twists. There were even a few who were trying to make a big splash.

"I'm tired of you complaining about how terrible this place is," his mom said. "It's time you gave this place a fair chance. I want you to go over there and make friends with those kids."

Wally was a little afraid to go. He didn't know any of those kids. He took one look at his mom and knew he had no choice. He gathered up his courage and went over to where the dolphins were playing.

"Those were some really cool tricks," he said. "My name is Wally and we just moved here. Do you mind if I hang out with you guys for a little while?"

"Sure thing," said Danny. "We're just seeing who can do the best flips and who can make the biggest splash. You can take a turn if you want. Watch how high I can jump," said Danny as he swam off under the water and did a really big jump.

"Nice one, Danny, but watch this splash," said David. He swam under the water as far as he could go and came up really fast and made the biggest splash of the day.

"Let's see if you can beat that," David said to Wally.

"That was pretty good," said Wally, "but I'll show you how to make a really big splash. Better get back if you don't want to get soaked." He took off and swam really deep. Wally came roaring up as fast as he could and soared out of the water, twisted on his side, and made the biggest splash the dolphins had ever seen.

"That was amazing, Wally! I've never seen such a big splash! Can you do it again?" asked Danny.

"Sure thing," said Wally, and he made an even bigger splash. For the next several hours, Wally taught the dolphins how to make really big splashes. David taught Wally a few tricks, and by the end of the day, Wally had made lots of new friends.

When Wally went home, he hugged his mom. "Thank you for making me go play with those kids. You were right, and I shouldn't have complained so much. I was just sad because I missed Willy and thought I would never have a best friend again. Those kids today were really nice, especially Danny and David. Maybe this place isn't so terrible after all," said Wally.

From then on, Wally was a lot happier because he stopped feeling sorry for himself and went out and did something about it.

Xander the x-ray fish was so angry that he swam right by his best friend Steve the stingray, mumbling "he makes me so mad!"

"What's wrong?" asked Steve the stingray.

"It's Graham. He makes me so mad I want to scream," said Xander.

"Was he making fun of your size again?" asked Steve.

"Yeah," said Xander. "I know, I know, he's a grouper and he's supposed to be big, and I'm an X-ray fish and I'm supposed to be small. I've heard it a million times. It's the size of your heart that matters and not the size of your body. I hate being small. You can't do things that everyone else can. Sometimes I think Graham is right. Maybe I'm not good for anything."

"That's not true and you know it," said Steve. "You're a great person. You have lots of friends and are always doing nice things for other people. You need to stop worrying about the things you can't do and appreciate the good things you can do. Just forget about Graham. I've got something really important to tell you. Remember last week when we heard those big kids talking about the Cave of Lights? We thought they were making it up because we spent all day looking for it and couldn't find it?"

"I remember," said Xander. "Wait a minute, are you saying it exists? It's real?"

"Not only is there a cave of lights, but I know exactly where it is. Want to go check it out?" asked Steve.

"Are you kidding? What are we waiting for? Let's go!" said Xander.

Xander jumped on Steve's back and they sped off to find the Cave of Lights. What they didn't know was that Graham was watching them and decided to follow. It was nearly an hour before they reached the Cave of Lights.

"Now, be really careful," said Steve. "The walls are pretty fragile, and any loud noise or banging into them could cause a cave-in."

"Steve, remember who you're talking to?" said Xander. "I'm barely two inches long. I could pound on the walls all day long and nothing would happen to them."

"Oh, yeah," said Steve, "sorry about that."

"That's okay," said Xander. "Let's go in and check it out!"

Xander and Steve slowly entered the cave. At first it was really dark and they couldn't see a thing. They started to wonder if they had the right place, but when they swam around the next bend, there it was— the cave opened up and it was filled with lights. It was beautiful.

"Wow, this is the coolest thing I've ever seen," said Xander. "The walls look like they have diamonds in them. This is unbelievable!" Xander started to say when he heard a huge roar followed by a big crash. They rushed to see what had happened. When they got to the front of the cave, there was a huge pile of rocks blocking the entrance. There was a noise coming from underneath the rocks, it sounded like a voice calling for help.

It was Graham, and he was trapped by a large rock. Graham told them how he had followed them and was going to play a little joke and try to scare them. When he started to make a scary noise, the roof shook and then fell on him before he could get out of the way. He was trapped and the rocks were too heavy to move.

Xander, being so small, was able to swim down to Graham. He didn't look so good, and Xander knew he had to do something. As he swam back up, Xander noticed a small space in the rocks that blocked the entrance.

"Steve, I'm going to try and squeeze through that little hole up top and go get some help," said Xander.

Xander was able to squeeze through the tiny hole and he raced home to get help. He told his dad what had happened and they quickly got the other parents and set off to save Graham.

When they reached the Cave of Lights, the parents worked together and quickly pulled the rocks off of Graham. He was so happy to be free, but Graham felt really bad for what he had done. As soon as he was free, he went to Xander and apologized.

"Xander, I know I tease you about your size, and I'm sorry," said Graham. "I just always thought, you know, the bigger the better. Now I know that is not true. If you weren't so small, I'd still be stuck in there. I'm sorry, and I promise to never make fun of your size again."

"That's okay, Graham," said Xander. He finally understood that it wasn't your body size but the size of your heart that made you a big person. He saved a life today, and that made Xander feel ten feet tall.

Yakkie the Yak

Yakkie loved to talk. She would talk to anyone that would listen. At first, everyone thought it was kind of cute, but then Yakkie took it to far. She would talk and talk and never give the other kids a chance to say anything. Yakkie started talking so much that her friends began making up excuses so they didn't have to listen to her.

One day on her way to school, Yakkie saw Chip the cheetah and called out to him. "Hi, Chip."

"Oh, hi, Yakkie," Chip answered. He was about to ask her how she was doing when Yakkie interrupted him and started talking and wouldn't stop.

"I'm doing just fine," began Yakkie. "Isn't it a great day today? I think the weather is just perfect this time of year. Did you know that it's supposed to be very hot later? We could go swimming in my pool after school if you want. Would you like to go swimming after school? We could swim and talk and…"

"Hold on, Yakkie," shouted Chip. "I don't think I can go swimming later. I have something else to do, something real important. Well, I'm late and really have to go now. Bye, Yakkie," said Chip, and he ran away before Yakkie started talking again.

That was strange, Yakkie thought. Why did Chip run away so fast? He probably forgot his homework and that's why he left in such a big hurry. He didn't want to be late for school. Yes, that must be it, thought Yakkie, and she continued on her way.

A few minutes later, she saw Samson the snake and called to him.

"Hi, Samson, how are you?" asked Yakkie, but before he could answer, she started talking again. "I'm doing fine. Isn't it a great day today? I think the weather is perfect this time of year. Did you know that it's supposed to be very hot later? We could go swimming in my pool after school if you want. Would you like to go swimming in my pool after school? We could swim and talk and…"

"Yakkie," shouted Samson. "I'm sorry but I can't go swimming with you later. I'm very busy right now and can't talk. Bye, Yakkie." Samson slithered away as fast as he could before Yakkie started talking again.

Now that's strange, thought Yakkie. Everyone was in such a hurry today. Nobody had the time to stop and talk. Yakkie continued on her way. She tried talking to Pam the puma and Iggy the iguana, but they all left in a hurry. Yakkie started to think that maybe everyone wasn't in a hurry. Maybe she did something wrong. After school, Yakkie went home and told her mom what had happened.

"Mom, I don't understand what's happened to all my friends," said Yakkie. "Every time I try to talk to them, they say they're busy and run away. I didn't say anything mean or bad. I just wanted to talk to them and invite them to come swimming with me. What did I do that was so bad? Why don't my friends like me anymore?" asked Yakkie as tears welled in her eyes.

"Oh, honey, don't cry," her mom said. "I think I know what the problem is and how to fix it. First, I need you to promise me that you'll listen to what I have to say with no interruptions, okay, sweetheart?"

"I promise I won't interrupt," said Yakkie. "What did I do wrong?" "Well, honey, I think the problem is that you talk too much and don't listen enough," her mom said. Yakkie was just about to interrupt, when her mom said, "Now hear me out. Before, when you told me what happened with your friends, I don't think you were listening to what you said."

"What do you mean, Mom?" asked Yakkie. "All I did was ask them if they wanted to go swimming."

"No," her mom said, "you asked those kids four questions and never gave them a chance to answer you. You probably would have kept on talking if they didn't stop you. A conversation is two people talking and two people listening. Lately, you've been doing all the talking, and your friends have been doing all the listening. That doesn't sound like a whole lot of fun for them. Perhaps try listening more and talking less."

Yakkie thought about what her mom had said, and she was right. She had been doing all the talking, and that wasn't very nice for her friends. Yakkie went to all her friends and told them that she was sorry and would try to be a better friend.

That day after school, the kids were just hanging out in the playground, talking. They couldn't believe it. They had been there for half an hour and other than "Hello," Yakkie had not said one word. She was actually letting the other kids talk. Maybe Yakkie can change, they thought.

From that day forward, Yakkie tried really hard to be a good listener. In fact, Yakkie became such a good listener that all the kids loved talking to her. This made Yakkie really happy, because she has lots of friends now, and it's all because she talks less and listens more.

Ziggy the Zebra

Zed and Zora loved their son, Ziggy, very much. They thought he was the most precious zebra in the world. Like all parents, they wanted the best for their child. They both worked very hard to give Ziggy the things they never had as children.

When Zed and Zora were kids, their families didn't have much money. They had a safe place to sleep and plenty of food to eat, but there wasn't a lot of money left over for other things. They never got big expensive presents or had fancy parties, but they did get a lot of love from their families.

Back then, most people had something called "family night." It was one night a week where they would get together as a family and play a game. They took turns picking the games they would play. Mom made a huge bowl of popcorn for all to share. Dad made our special Family Fun Night drink. We called it "Grape-o-licious." It was one-half grape juice and one-half ginger ale and one hundred percent delicious. They talked and laughed well into the night. Some nights, they had so much fun that they didn't stop playing until midnight. Yes, those were really great times, remembered Zed and Zora.

They wanted to show Ziggy how much they loved him. They both worked hard at their jobs so they could buy Ziggy the things they never had.

Ziggy's birthday was a month away, and they decided to throw him a big fancy party with lots of presents. This was going to cost a lot of money, but Ziggy was worth it. They would have to work a little extra overtime to pay for it all, but that was okay.

Ziggy loved his parents very much. They gave him everything he ever wanted. He knew how happy it made them to buy him nice things. He had lots of fancy games, but his parents never had time to play with him. They were always too tired from working so much to play with him. Ziggy didn't want to spend every minute of the day with his parents, but a little time would be nice. Ziggy knew if he told his parents how he felt, it would hurt their feelings, so he decided not to say anything. Ziggy knew his parents loved him, even if they didn't have enough time to spend with him.

One night at dinner, his mom said, "Ziggy, the next two weeks, your dad and I have to work some extra nights so we can make your birthday special. We're counting on you to be good while we are at work."

Ziggy couldn't believe what he was hearing. "Yeah, sure, whatever. You're never home anyway," came out of Ziggy's mouth before he could stop himself.

"Hey, that's not a very nice thing to say to your mother," said Zed who started to get angry at Ziggy's lack of respect. "Now apologize to your mother for being fresh. Don't you understand we are working extra hard for you?"

Ziggy was really nervous, and he knew his parents were going to be mad, but he just had to tell them the truth about how he felt.

"Mom, I'm sorry for being fresh," said Ziggy. Then he cleared his throat and gathered up his courage and added, "Please don't be mad, but I really don't want a big fancy party for my birthday. I mean, it's nice, and I do like the presents, but it's not worth it if you have to work more. We never get to spend any time together. I'd rather do something fun with you for my birthday than have a big fancy party."

Ziggy's parents felt terrible. They always tried to do the right thing. They just wanted to be good parents and give Ziggy the things they never had.

"Oh, Ziggy, we're sorry. We didn't know you felt this way," his mom said.

"You know we love you," said his dad. "We only want the best for you."

"I know you were only trying to do nice things for me," said Ziggy. "Now don't get me wrong. I still love presents, but I love being with you more," said Ziggy as he hugged his parents.

His dad said, "Ziggy, I know the perfect present for your birthday."

"Dad, didn't you hear me? I don't want big fancy presents," said Ziggy.

"It's not expensive," his dad said. "It's perfect!"

It was his birthday and Ziggy was excited to open the perfect present his dad talked about. When Ziggy opened the prefect present, the only thing in the box was a piece of paper. What kind of perfect present is this? thought Ziggy until he read the paper titled "Family Night." It explained all the fun family things his parents did as kids, and they promised to play those same games with Ziggy. His dad was right— this was the perfect present!

From then on, they had family night once a week. Ziggy is really happy he told his parents how he felt, so now he gets to spend more time with them. Zed and Zora are happier and better parents, because they realized that the best gift they could give their child wasn't a big expensive toy but just to spend more time with him.

About the Author

Joe Conroy's two children, Joseph and Jessica, were his inspiration for many of the stories. He currently lives in Florida with his beautiful wife, Kelly. Joe is a full-time author who spends most days writing on the beach. When not writing, he enjoys playing guitar and reading to local elementary students.